Viz Graphic Novel

FLAME OF RECCA

Vol. 4

Action Edition

Story and Art by
Nobuyuki Anzai

Flame of Recca
Vol. 4
Action Edition

Story and Art by
Nobuyuki Anzai

English Adaptation/Lance Caselman
Translation/Joe Yamazaki
Touch-up & Lettering/Kelle Han
Graphics & Cover Design/Sean Lee
Editor/Eric Searleman

Managing Editor/Annette Roman
Editor-in-Chief/William Flanagan
Production Manager/Noboru Watanabe
Sr. Director of Licensing & Acquisitions/Rika Inouye
VP of Sales & Marketing/Liza Coppola
Sr. VP of Editorial/Hyoe Narita
Publisher/Seiji Horibuchi

Printed in Canada

Published by VIZ, LLC
P.O. Box 77064
San Francisco, CA 94107

Action Edition
10 9 8 7 6 5 4 3 2 1
First printing, January 2004

Viz Graphic Novel

FLAME OF RECCA™

Vol. 4

Story & Art by Nobuyuki Anzai

Contents

ANNIHILATE THE HOKAGE NINGUN!!

KILL! KILL THEM!!

I'LL GET YOU TO A SAFE PLACE ...

DON'T BE AFRAID RECCA ....

Part Thirty: Mikagami and Kaoru

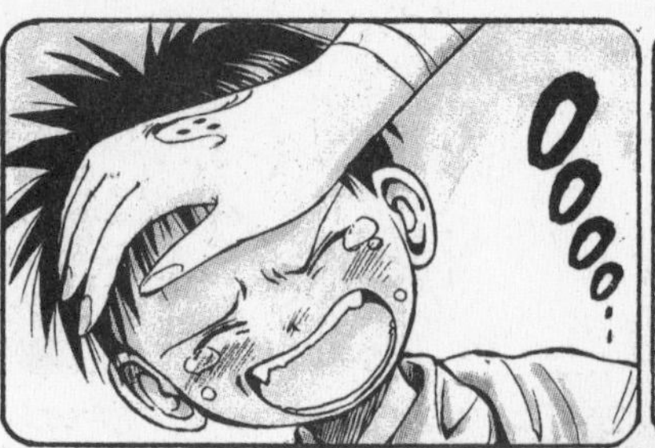

HOKAGE HIJUTSU

JIKŪ RYŪRI

FWASH

SHWRR

KRASH

I HOPE THAT THE TIME YOU DRIFT TO...
WILL BE PEACEFUL AND FREE OF WARS...

GOOD BYE ...
MY BELOVED RECCA ...

PLINK

HUH !!?
PLIP...
SO YOU'RE FINALLY AWAKE, EH, HOT SHOT!!

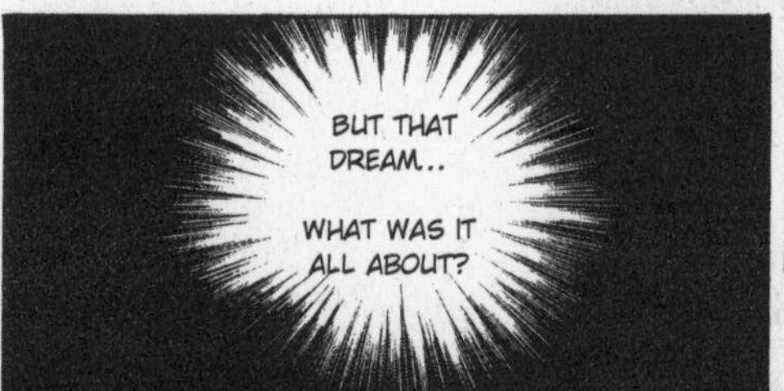

MEANWHILE, THIRD FLOOR: KAORU'S ROOM
I'LL SHOW YOU THE REAL POWER OF THE KŌGON ANKIN.
KREK
CHING
!?
TRANS-FORM!! KŌGON ANKIN MODE 2-- RYU, THE DRAGON !!
KUSARI GAMA !!!

THE WEAPON ... CHANGED?
WUP
IT'S BEEN A WHILE SINCE I'VE HAD TO TRANSFORM IT.
CONSIDER IT A COMPLIMENT, SOMETHING TO BRAG ABOUT.♪
WUP
KŌGON ANKIN (ATTRIBUTE: GOLD)
A WEAPON FORGED BY ALCHEMY FROM AN INTETSU METEOR. IT HAS FIVE MODES OR FACES.
HERE WE GO!!
CHANK
HA!
HYAH ♡
WUP

!?

SKEESH

SKEESH

SKEESH

SKEESH

HEY!
CHING
WAP
YOU'RE THE SECOND PERSON TO EVER MAKE ME BLEED LIKE THIS.
SLURP
NOW *YOU* CAN BRAG, KID!
WOOP
BUT YOU SEE....
CHAK
WEE--- THIS IS JUST LIKE PRO-WRESTLING!
A CHAIN DEATH MATCH. IT'S WING.
WOOM

MODE 3--
KYOKU,
EXTREME
!!
OO BASAMI! THE BIG SCIS-SORS!!
KLAK KLAK KLAK
KAK
!
WHAP
KLANK...

HE'S NOT JUST A CHILD...

HE COMPENSATES FOR HIS LACK OF BODILY STRENGTH WITH THAT WEAPON!

GRIN

GO AHEAD! PICK UP YOUR SWORD!!

I'LL WAIT FOR YOU!

HE'S NOT ATTACKING!?

THE FIVE FACES REPRESENT THE FIVE FORMS!

ICHI (1)

NI (2)

SAN (3)

KAORU'S LESSON

THE KŌGON ANKIN HAS FIVE MODES.

THINK YOU'LL LIVE TO SEE THEM ALL?

CHAKI

YES, BUT I'M NOT SO SURE YOU WILL.

CHING!
CHANG
KLANG
SLASH
AH!!
WHUK
WUMP..
UNH ...!
OUR SWORDSMANSHIP IS MATCHED, BUT...
KRESH
MY WOUND IS A DISADVANTAGE ...

GRR
GRR
THAT'S WHAT RECCA WOULD SAY....
WHY AM I THINKING OF HIM NOW! HOW UNPLEASANT.....

EMBAR-RASSED, MORON? ♡
NEENER NEENER! STUPID MIKAGAMI!

EVEN AFTER HE WAS HURT IN OUR FIGHT, HE NEVER LOST THE FIRE IN HIS EYES...
FWAP
HFF
HFF
BUT WHAT WOULD HE DO IN THIS SITUA-TION?

IT'S BEEN FUN, BUDDY!!
CHEEN
CHAR
BUT I GOTTA RUN!!

MODE 4--MIKAZUKI, THE CRESCENT MOON!!
BOOM

I WON'T LOSE ...TO THIS BRAT ...
OR TO YOU, RECCA !!

BOOMERANG!!
FWUP
FWUP
VEEEEN
WHAT ...!
FWIK
WHERE IS HE ...?
FROM WHERE ...
WILL HE ATTACK ?
ENSU!!
CHAK...

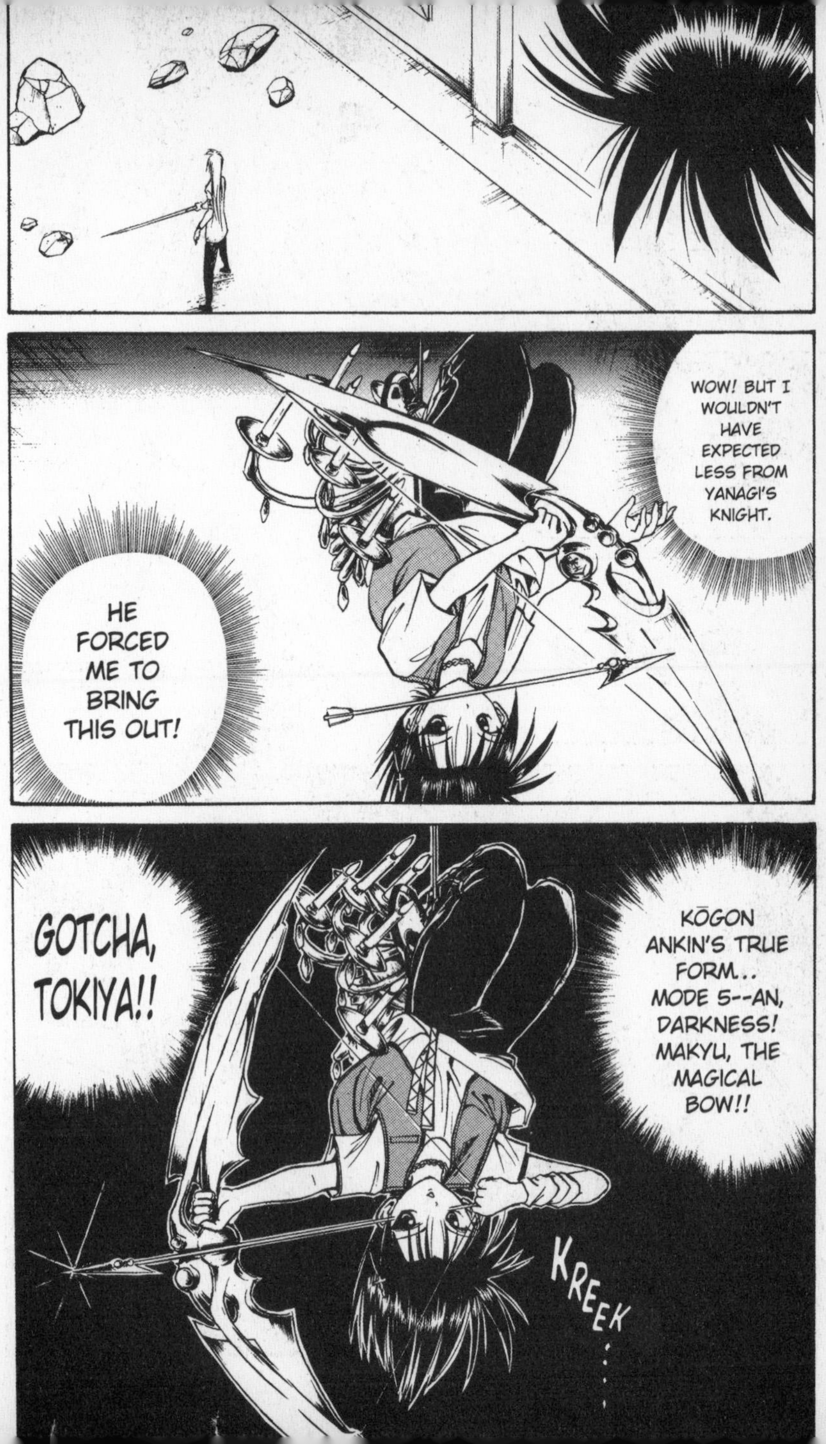

KŌGON ANKIN'S TRUE FORM.. MODE 5--AN, DARKNESS! MAKYU, THE MAGICAL BOW!!

KREEK...

GOTCHA, TOKIYA!!

!?
FOOOOOOO
IT'S THE WATER SWORD !
HE'S TRYING TO CONCEAL HIMSELF ....
FOOOO
VAPOR !?
FWP...
YOU UNDER-ESTIMATE ME...
TWANG
WHAP
THERE YOU ARE!!
CHUNK

AAAAAH!

TMP
WHOA
!
WUMP

FWIP
I
WIN.

THE
VAPOR
DIDN'T
CONCEAL
ME.
◁REAL▷
◁FAKE▷
IT
DISGUISED
THE EFFIGY
I MADE
FROM SOME
OF ENSUI'S
WATER.
I
DISCOVERED
YOUR
POSITION BY
THE PATH OF
THE ARROW.
ENSUI
(ATTRIBUTES:
WATER)
THIS SWORD CAN
TRANSMUTE
LIQUID INTO A
BLADE, OR ANY
OTHER SHAPE.

I OWE YOU
FOR LETTING
ME PICK UP
MY SWORD.
YOU CAN
LIVE. NOW
DROP YOUR
WEAPON
AND GO!

HIF
....
SNIFF
.....
UWAAH
...
SOB
SOB
OINK PLOINK
UWAAAAAH
WONG WONG

GIRLIE-BOY!! SISSY!!
WAPPH
WAPPH
YOU BIG JERK!!!
I LEARNED THAT TRICK FROM RECCA!!
IF YOU LOST TO ME,
THEN YOU'D HAVE A HARD TIME AGAINST HIM!
SKRERF
HEY!
PIANO WIRE
I DIDN'T LOSE!! SEE YOU LATER, SISSY!
WE'LL DO THIS AGAIN-- REAL SOON!!
ANY TIME ...

Part Thirty-One: Fury

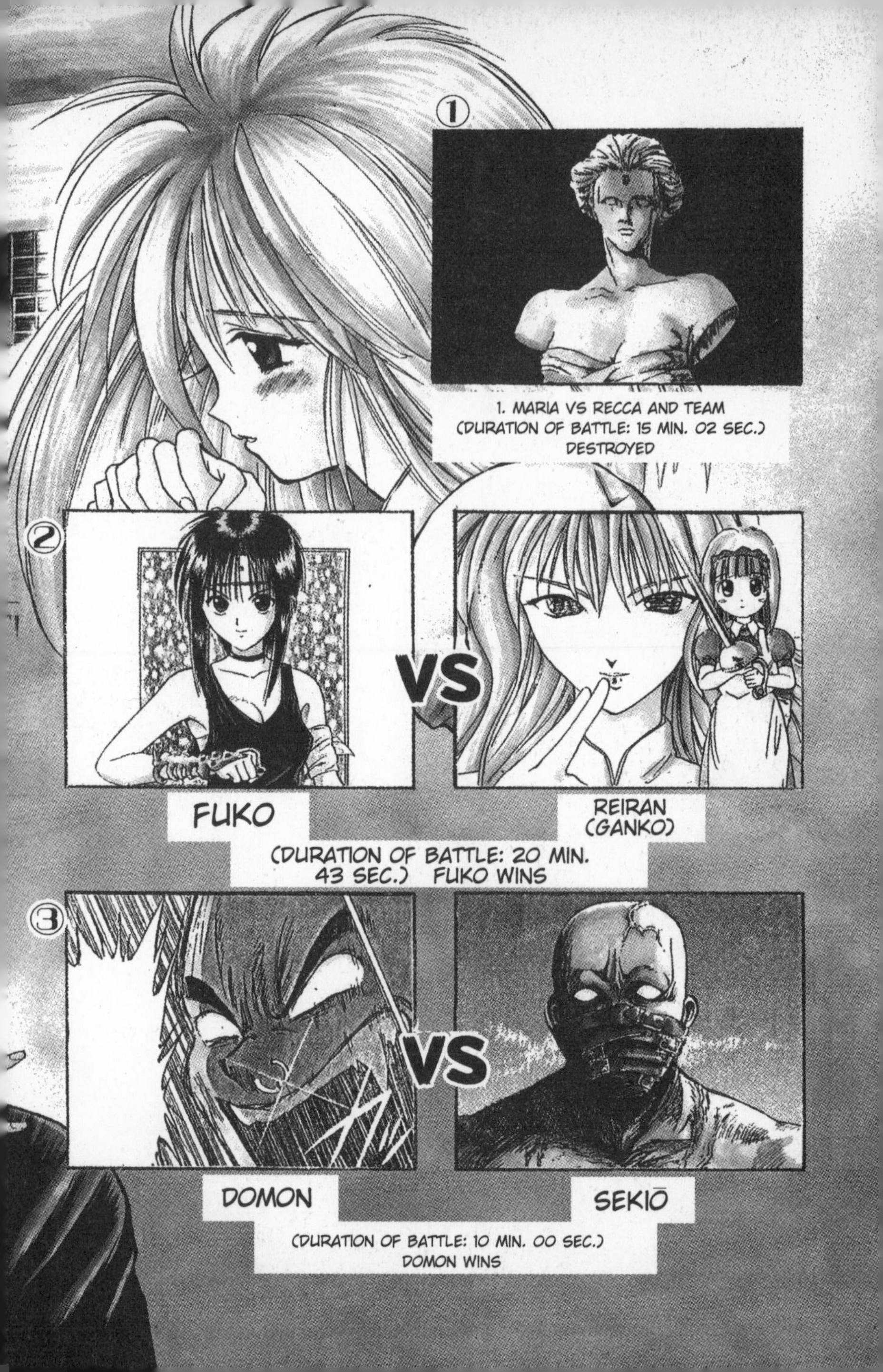

1. MARIA VS RECCA AND TEAM
(DURATION OF BATTLE: 15 MIN. 02 SEC.)
DESTROYED

FUKO

VS

REIRAN
(GANKO)

(DURATION OF BATTLE: 20 MIN.
43 SEC.) FUKO WINS

DOMON

SEKIŌ

(DURATION OF BATTLE: 10 MIN. 00 SEC.)
DOMON WINS

Part Thirty-One:
Fury
④
VS
TOKIYA MIKAGAMI
KAORU
(BATTLE TIME: 32 MIN. 55 SEC.)—DRAW

CHAK
CHAK
DARN! IT'S LOCKED !!

OH NO, FUKO'S SILKY SMOOTH HAND'S ARE ALL CUT UP!
YAY!
COOL! NOSE RINGS!
IT WON'T OPEN... EVEN I CAN'T BUDGE IT!
ERK
ERK
STOP

THOOM

NEENER
NEENER
烈火の炎
~FLAME OF RECCA~

RECCA
...

YOU'RE HIDING YOUR EMOTIONS, BUT I KNOW...
YOU'VE NEVER BEEN SO ANGRY BEFORE...

I'VE KNOWN YOU FOR SO LONG.

WAP

OOF !!

DO IT AGAIN! SHE'S A SMART ALEC!

I'VE NEVER WAILED ON SOMEONE THIS SMALL.

THIS IS MESSED UP.

I'LL KICK YOUR LITTLE BUTT!!

TAKE IT EASY, DUDE...

TMP TMP

TMP

KSSST
WHO'RE YOU!?

I'LL ASK THE QUESTIONS!!

WHY ARE YOU PANSIES PICKING ON LITTLE KIDS!?

SHE'S A GIRL, COWARDS!!

RECCA...

THOSE JUNIOR HIGH BOYS BEAT HIM TO A PULP BUT...

FSSS...

UNH...I NEVER KNEW YOU WERE A QUINTUPLET, FUKO...

UNFAIRNESS ALWAYS INFURIATED YOU....

...IT SCARES ME... I CAN ALMOST FEEL THE HEAT OF YOUR RAGE MYSELF...

VWMMMM

KREE
IT'S ABOUT TIME....

I'VE BEEN WAITING FOR YOU FOUR. ♡
YOU STINKING RATS!!

...
GULP
MOKU-REN!!

YOU ...
YOU ALMOST KILLED MR. TATESAKO'S WIFE.

HUH?
SHE DIDN'T DIE? AW, SHUCKS ...

I MUST HAVE MISSED HER BRAINS! HEE HEE HEE....
TWITCH

HEY, YOU! THE GIRL WITH SHORT HAIR! MIND IF I KILL YOU?
KLIK
HOW 'BOUT YOU, LITTLE GIRL?
I'LL GET TO YOU BOYS LATER...♪

LADIES FIRST, YOU KNOW!!
I FIND SLAUGHTER TO BE AN EXCELLENT FORM OF EXERCISE. REALLY GETS THE BLOOD PUMPING. ♡

AND IT'S SO MUCH FUN!
GYAHAHAHAHAHAHA!!

WHERE DID THEY DIG UP THIS NAUSEATING PIECE OF WORK?
ALMOST MAKES YOU MISS TOKIYA.

YOU...
WUR---
HEY, WAIT A SECOND!

WE'LL NEED A LITTLE BACKGROUND MUSIC.
Pi Pi
YOU'LL LOVE IT! ♡
TRACK ONE, PLAY!!!
WM-MM
AAAAH
AAAAAAH
GYAAAH

WHAT IS THIS? ARE THOSE SCREAMS ...!?
AAGHHH
AAAAA
MY EARS ...
IT'S HORRIBLE!
AH
AAAAH
......
AAAAH
ZOOOOOOOO!!

AAAAAH!!!

SKRFFF

SKRFFF

SKRFFF

AAAAAAAH!!!

...THAT VOICE....

OH NO...

HEE HEE...

PRINCESS...!

A HUMAN EXPERIMENT.
JUST A LITTLE ELECTRIC SHOCK.
KUREI'S GONNA EXTRACT HER POWERS.
THEY'RE DOING ALL SORTS OF TESTS ON HER.
I'D LOVE TO WATCH IT LIVE, BUT I HAVE TO DEAL WITH YOU GUYS!!
SO I'LL JUST KILL YOU QUICKLY AND GO WATCH THE FUN!!
!
BOOM

FYOOOOO

KUREI ...

MOKUREN OF KODAMA, THE WOOD SPIRIT !!!

IMPALING TIME!! FEEL FREE TO SCREAM!!

KODAMA
(ATTRIBUTE: WOOD)

A TALISMAN SPHERE ENABLES HIM TO HOST PLANTS IN HIS BODY, AND WIELD THEM AS LETHAL WEAPONS.

I'M OVER HERE!
MOKUREN !!
DON'T FORGET THE RULES !!
HOW DARE YOU IGNORE ME!!?
HEY
....
KLIK

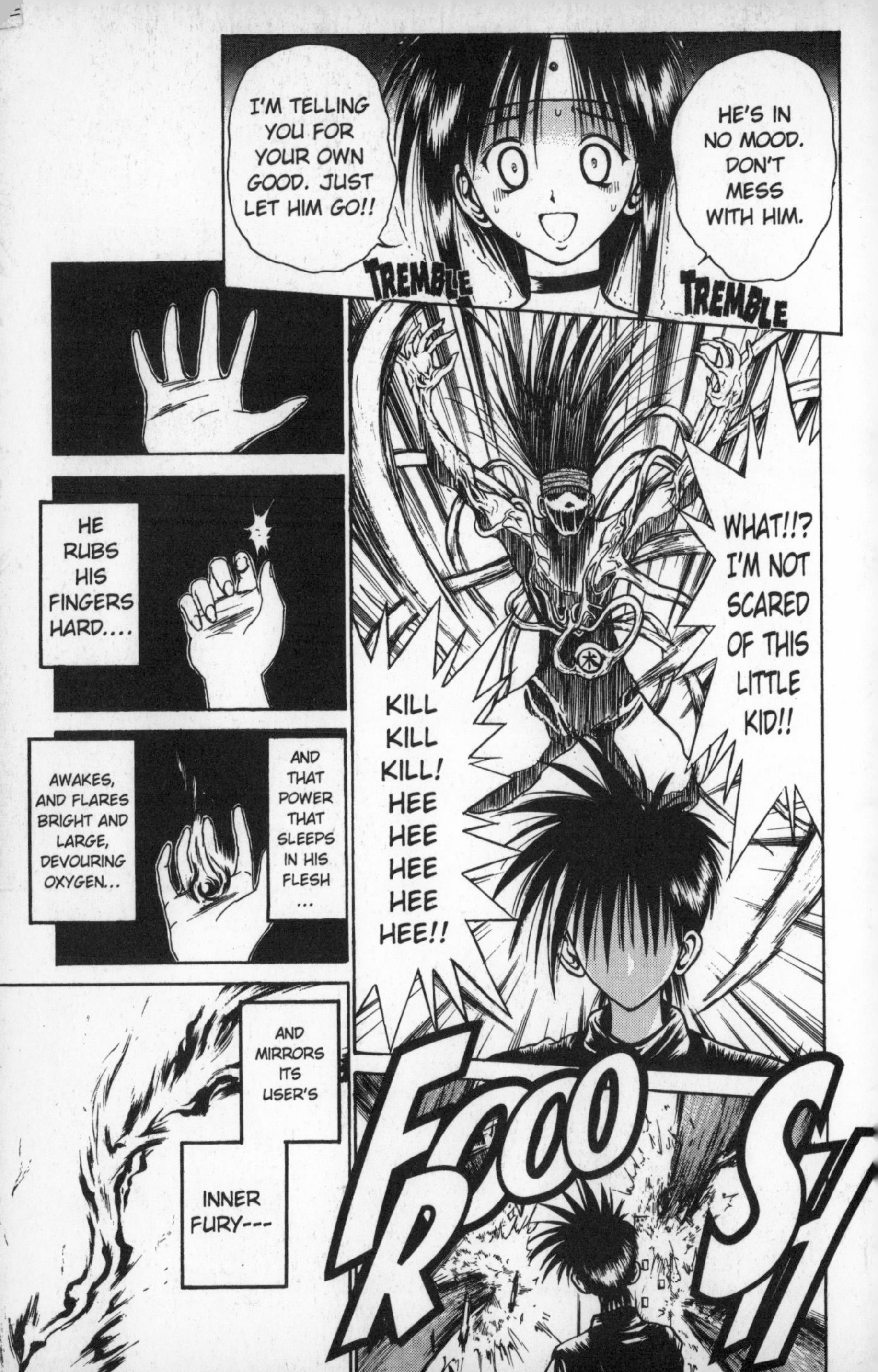
HE'S IN NO MOOD. DON'T MESS WITH HIM.
I'M TELLING YOU FOR YOUR OWN GOOD. JUST LET HIM GO!!
TREMBLE
TREMBLE
WHAT!!? I'M NOT SCARED OF THIS LITTLE KID!!
KILL KILL KILL! HEE HEE HEE HEE HEE HEE!!
HE RUBS HIS FINGERS HARD....
AND THAT POWER THAT SLEEPS IN HIS FLESH ...
AWAKES, AND FLARES BRIGHT AND LARGE, DEVOURING OXYGEN...
AND MIRRORS ITS USER'S
INNER FURY---
FROOOSH

FLAME OF RECCA !!
CLEAR MY PATH !!!

EEYAAAAAAH!!!

FWOOOSH

AAAAA-AAAH! IT BURNS! MY BODY BURNS!!

FIRE? LIKE KUREI'S --- IT'S KUREI FLAME !!

I'VE NEVER SEEN HIM SO...

FURIOUS.

NOW FOR KUREI!

HE WAS JUST A SPEED-BUMP!!

GYAAAAAAA

Part Thirty-Two: Kurenai

AAAAA-
AAAH! IT BURNS! MY BODY BURNS !!
FIRE! CON-
SUMING ME!!!
FWERRRR
AAAA-
AAAH !!
SLUUCK
FLURRP
KLUP KLUP
...
HA!
FWUMP
HAH ...
HAAAA ....
STOP
RECCA ...

LET'S GO.
WAIT !!
HFF
KRERK
I WON'T FORGET THIS PAIN...THIS HATE....
HFF
RECCA ...
I'D REALLY ENJOY IMPALING YOU!!
HFF
HFF

BUT YOU'LL NEVER SURVIVE KUREI'S FLAME!!
YOUR'S IS NOTHING NEXT TO HIS!! IT'LL DO TO YOU WHAT YOU'VE DONE TO ME!!
HAH
KUREI'S FLAMES ?
WA HA HA HA HA
HE MAKES FLAMES TOO!?
STOP
CHING
B2 B1 1
WHRAA
3 2

MASTER KUREI ---
WE'VE PUSHED THE SUBJECT'S PAIN TO LEVEL 6.
SHE'S IN THE DANGER ZONE! SHE COULD DIE!!
PERHAPS WE SHOULD LESSEN THE INTENSITY !!!

KEEP GOING!!

SHE WANTS TO SURVIVE, IT'S THE MOST PRIMAL DRIVE...
WHEN SHE BELIEVES SHE'S GOING TO DIE, SHE'LL USE HER HEALING POWERS.

B-BUT ...
YOU'RE SUPPOSED TO BE EXPERTS! APPLY AS MUCH PAIN AS SHE CAN BEAR WITHOUT DYING.

REMEMBER, THIS IS FOR SCIENCE.
THERE'S NO ROOM FOR SYMPATHY.

AND NOW ...
I HAVE GUESTS TO GREET.
RECCA ...
WRRRR
THE BATTLE WITH MOKUREN WAS QUITE A SHOW.
BUT NOW THE ELEVATOR WILL BECOME...
FWEERRR
YOUR COFFIN.
CHING...
DIE !!
HRUK

!
READY,
SET...

FWASH

SNRK
UNH ... YOU ....
KNEW ?
DUH !
I KNEW YOU'D TRY SOMETHING SNEAKY.
HRSSK
AND NOW ...
IT'S TIME WE SETTLED THIS!!
RAAAAAAAH!!

KRAK
KRAAK
KRAAK
AAAAARRGH

WHACK
FWOOOO...
MY FLAME ---
IS GONE TOO...
BURNED OUT ...?

HAH,
WE TIED!!
WUP

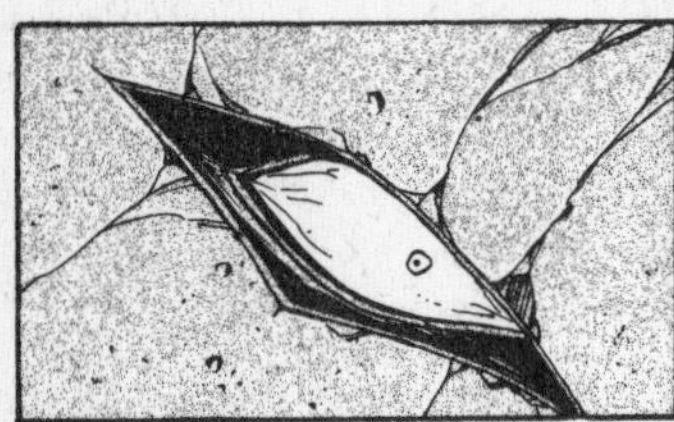

HEH... AMAZING. THE FLAME'S ...
EVEN MORE POWERFUL THAN BEFORE! SPLENDID ......

LET PRINCESS GO!

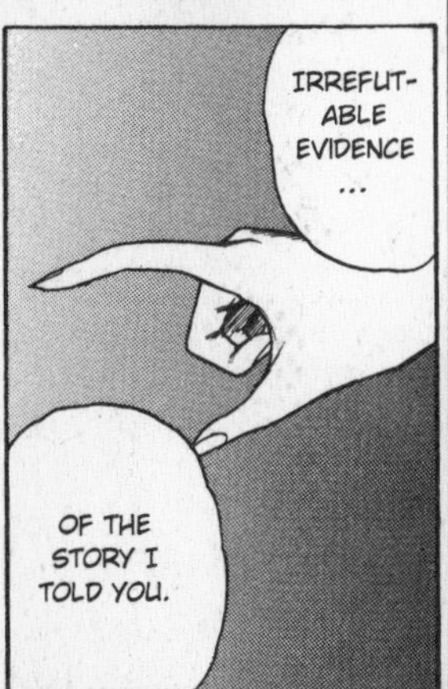
IRREFUT-ABLE EVIDENCE ...
OF THE STORY I TOLD YOU.

THAT HOLE IN YOUR CHEEK UNDER THE BANDAGE!!

IT'S A KNIFE WOUND!

DON'T YOU REMEMBER? I GAVE YOU THAT!
IT'S TRUE ...

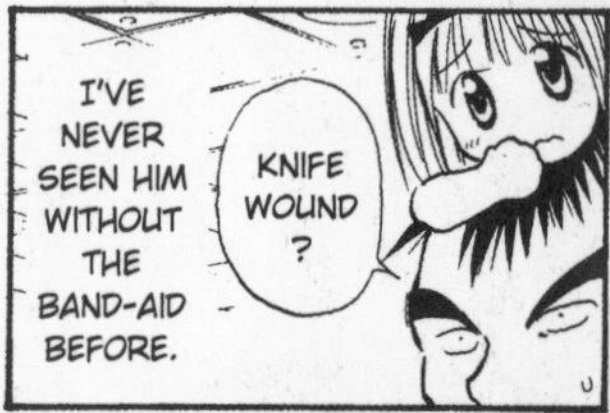
KNIFE WOUND ?
I'VE NEVER SEEN HIM WITHOUT THE BAND-AID BEFORE.

SWAP
DARN!

DON'T YOU SEE!? YOU WEREN'T BORN IN THIS AGE!!
YOU'RE A HOKAGE NINJA OF THE SENGOKU ERA WHO WAS SET ADRIFT THROUGH TIME!!

I'M STILL GONNA WASTE YOU!!!

RECCA ---
FWK
FWK
FWK
FWK
IF YOU HADN'T DRIFTED TO THE SAME TIME AS I...
IF YOU HADN'T MET YANAGI SAKO-SHITA...
IF YOU HADN'T MET KAGEHOSHI ...
FWOOSH
YOUR FORTUNE IS TRAGIC.
YOU COULD HAVE LIVED...

I REPEAT !!

PREPARE FOR EMERGENCY !!

Part Thirty-Three:
Living Flame

FWAP
AN ANGEL OF...
FIRE?
...
BEAUTIFUL ...
KYAAAAAAAA

BOOM
AAAAA
...
BOOM
BOOM
OOOOOOOOOOOH!!
KA-DOOM

KSSS
......!
WHAT THE HELL IS THAT FIERY FREAK!?
THE STEEL PLATE MELTED LIKE IT WAS WAX...
GEEZ, IF WE GET HIT BY THAT THING ...
THERE WON'T EVEN BE ASHES LEFT!!

WHOA !!

HFF
HFF
I'M... SCARED ...

DOMON'S AFRAID TOO...

I'VE NEVER FELT SUCH FEAR IN MY LIFE...

THAT BITCH...IS DEADLY!!

KURENAI
...

INCINERATE THAT LITTLE GIRL.

REIRAN-- I MEAN, GANKO! I'M VERY DISAPPOINTED IN YOU.
IT'S ONE THING TO LOSE, BUT TO BECOME A TRAITOR ...?

GLOG GLOG
YOU'RE LUCKY!
YOU'RE GOING TO SEE MOMMY.
HAHAHAHAHAHAHAH
MASTER KUREI ....
CAN'T MOVE MY FEET ... FROM FEAR ...
GANKO.
I'M FROZEN!!
STOP!!

!
Y...
YAAA-AAH
YES!!
STOP
RECCA...

YOU MADE A CHILD DO YOUR DIRTY WORK!!
YOU KILLED YOUR SERVANTS WHO FAILED YOU! YOU'RE AN EVIL SCUMBAG, KUREI!
YOU USE YOUR POWER TO CRUSH THE WEAK!
YOU GET WHAT YOU WANT, NO MATTER WHAT IT COST OTHERS! DO YOU THINK YOU'RE GOD!
NO MORE, YOU PIG!!
FWOOSH

YOU CAN'T CONTROL EVERY-BODY WITH FEAR!
I'M NOT AFRAID OF YOU!!
I'LL FIGHT YOU!! C'MON!!

I WON'T LOSE...
SKRAK
SKRAK
I'LL TOAST YOU!

......
TOAST ME? WITH THAT LITTLE FLICKER OF A FLAME?

KURENAI!
DISINTE-GRATE HIM!

FWOOOM
WHAT ...!?
FUJIN WIELDER ---
THAT'S RIGHT, RECCA ...
WE WON'T LOSE ...!!
FUKO KIRISAWA !

HAI-YA!!
SUPERHUMAN STRENGTH--- DOMON ISHIJIMA!!
WHO'S AFRAID!?

SLASH
THAT'S RIGHT, MASK BOY.
I WON'T TOLERATE YOUR TYRANNY ANY LONGER.
TOKIYA, YOU SHOW-OFF!!
HE'S HERE...
KWAAAA
THE FLAME...
TAKE THIS!

A SHINOBI, PLEDGED TO YANAGI SAKOSHITA!

RECCA HANABISHI !!

Part Thirty-Four:
Man-Eating Devil
HELP

SMIRK...
KURENAI ISN'T SOLID FLESH. SHE'S MERELY A FLAME IN HUMAN FORM.
AND YOU CAN'T CUT OR BURN FLAMES?
HMPH
GRRR !!

HOW SAD.
HEY! THAT HURT, YOU JERK!!
STOP PLAYING AROUND !!
KOFF KOFF
THAT DOES IT!!
KRAK
RECCA, WAIT!
YOUR RAGE IS AFFECTING YOUR JUDGMENT.
THE ENEMY IS STRONG! DO YOU WANT TO SAVE YANAGI OR SATISFY YOUR ANGER?
AS ALWAYS ...

YOU WON'T SAVE MISS YANAGI BY PLAYING FAIR!

LISTEN! *SORCERY* REQUIRES A *SORCERER.*
AND A FLAME REQUIRES A WIELDER. IF WE CAN'T BEAT THE FLAME, WE HAVE TO TAKE OUT ITS SOURCE!
Y-YOU'RE RIGHT... GOTCHA, TOKIYA BABY.
YOU'RE ASKING FOR A FAT LIP, BUB...
KRK KRK
AHA!
TAKING OUT THE TRASH GETS RID OF THE STINK!
OOO OOO
IGNORE KURENAI!
HE'S OUR TARGET!!
ALL RIGHT!!

SPREAD OUT!!!

WHOOM

HEH...HE'S RIGHT, THIS IS NOT A GAME. NO NEED TO WORRY...
KURENAI!! YOU MAY HUNT ONE PREY!!

KILL !!
KYAAAA AAAA
FOOOM
HEH... SO...
YOU FANCY RECCA!
!!
WOOSH
C'MON, HOT STUFF !!

WHU
KA
DOM
8
FWOOM

I'LL DEAL WITH HER... GET KUREI!
AAARGHH!
FUJIN!!

KURENAI WENT AFTER RECCA BECAUSE ...
SHASH
SHE RECOGNIZED THAT HE IS THE STRONGEST.
GEN-JUTSU (ILLUSION)
TMP
HEH... YOU WIMPS DIDN'T EVEN REGISTER.

SHUT YOUR PIE HOLE!!
I CAN HANDLE YOU THREE WITHOUT KURENAI!!
KRAK

AAAAGH !!
FWUMP
DOMON!!
CHIK
ONE DOWN ...

TOO FAST...
KOFF
TWO DOWN...

TOKIYA...
WHA--!!
!?
WUMP

AND GIRLS ARE NO EXCEPTION!

FUKO !!
GANKO ... RUN ...
FWUMP
THAT MAKES FOUR...
YOU FOOLS MISCALCULATED DISASTROUSLY!
SKREE
SKREE
YOU UNDERESTIMATED KUREI! I'M FAR MORE POWERFUL THAN KURENAI
SKREE
YOUR STUPID ***COORDINATED ATTACK*** COULDN'T HURT ME!!
HOW BORING... KURENAI! BURN THEM UP, POLITELY.
MAKE THEM, THEIR SHAME, AND THEIR FOOLISHNESS DISAPPEAR FOR GOOD.

HOLD ON...
THE GAMES NOT QUITE OVER YET!!
HE CAN STAND !?
IMPOSSIBLE! HE WAS CONSUMED BY KURENAI'S FLAMES?
YOU CANNOT BURN A FLAME...
AND RECCA, A FLAME-WIELDER, POSSESSES A HIGH TOLERANCE AGAINST FIRE...

WHOOOM
THIS CHILD SHALL RISE AGAIN AND AGAIN FOR HIS PRINCESS,
WITH NO FEAR OF DEATH....
MISS YANAGI...

!!
THAT VOICE ...!!
THAT IS A SHINOBI!
KAGERO ...!!

烈火の炎
~FLAME OF RECCA~
SNURP

Part Thirty-Five:
Eight-Headed Doom
KAGERŌ
...

IT HAS BEEN A LONG TIME. BUT WHY THE MASK,
KUREI? IT DOES NOT SUIT YOU.
YOU ALWAYS APPEAR OUT OF NOWHERE, KAGEHOSHI.
SHADOW WORLD STONE,
EIKAI GYOKU (ATTRIBUTE = SHADOW)
THE POWER TO SEE THINGS FROM AFAR, TO ME (FAR EYE) AND KAGE IRI (SHADOW PORTAL), THE ABILITY TO MOVE FROM ONE SHADOW TO ANOTHER.
SKRU..
JUST ONE OF THE TRIALS RECCA MUST OVERCOME.
BOOO
BY USING THIS I CAN MOVE FROM SHADOW TO SHADOW.
IT WAS DIFFICULT PENETRATING THE FORCE-FIELD THAT KUREI SET AROUND THIS MANSION.
THE SITUATION IS AS BAD AS I'D IMAGINED.

SO THAT IS KUREI'S FLAME...
I WONDER HOW MANY FIRE-WIELDERS OF THE PAST COULD HAVE PRODUCED ITS LIKE.
AND COULD CONTROL IT AT WILL!
BRILLIANT.
KRK...

NOTHING...

REMOVE YOUR TEKKŌ! (FOREARM GUARD)

MY TEKKŌ?
WHY?
IT IS A SEAL.
THAT TEKKŌ PREVENTS THE ENERGY OF TH JETSUSHA'S FLAME FROM ACCIDENTALLY DISCHARGING.
THE ENERGY IS OF IMMEASURABLE POWER.
YOU MUST HAVE HAD IT SINCE YOU WERE A CHILD.
WHEN YOU REMOVE IT, YOUR HIDDEN POWERS WILL BE UNLEASHED!!
BUT WITHOUT THE TEKKŌ, IT IS POSSIBLE FOR YOUR OWN FLAME TO CONSUME YOU...
SINCE YOU ARE ALREADY PREPARED TO LOSE YOUR LIFE...
TAKE THE RISK!

HA ...
HA HA

HA HA HA HA HA! GREAT !!
I LIKE THAT WAY OF THINKING !!!

WHY DO YOU ALWAYS WEAR THAT THING, RECCA?
KLAK

HEE HEE! IT MAKES ME FEEL WARM AND SAFE!
AS THOUGH I HAD A MOTHER.
I GET NERVOUS WITHOUT IT!!
HMM ... WEIRD KID.

SO, WHEN I RELEASED MY FLAMES ...
THIS THING ALWAYS PROTECTED ME.
THANKS !

TAKE GOOD CARE OF IT, OKAY?
WHOA
FWAP

FWOOSH
WOW!
SOME-THING INSIDE OF ME IS ABOUT TO ...
EXPLODE!!
YOU REMOVED THE SEAL!? FOOL!!
AAAAAGH
DEAR GOD...
WHUM
PLEASE PROTECT MY CHILD!!
EVEN I WOULDN'T REMOVE MY TEKKŌ! IT MEANS CERTAIN DEATH!!
UGH!
BUZZ

FWOOM!!
WHAT'S HAPPENING !?
BOOM

FWOOSH
WOOM
BOOM
IT'S...
THE SOURCE OF RECCA'S FLAME!!
BOOM
BOOM
BABIN

MY ARM'S BURNING UP! AAAGH!!

TSSS ....

KSSSSS

YEEE-OWWW !!

WHO OOM

FWAK

FWOOSH

RAAAAAWR

IT ... CAN'T BE ...

HOW CAN HE... POSSESS SUCH A GREAT FLAME!? WHAT MONSTERS SLEEP WITHIN HIM!!
HOW CAN IT BE!?

KRASH
THE EIGHT-HEADED DRAGON ...
THE FLAME OF YAMATA !!

FWOOM
THIS IS HIS TRUE POWER !?

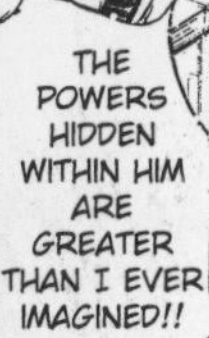
THE POWERS HIDDEN WITHIN HIM ARE GREATER THAN I EVER IMAGINED!!

ACCORDING TO THE ANCIENT SCROLLS, THERE WERE MANY TYPES OF FLAMES IN THE PAST! THE LION, THE SNAKE, THE HAWK...
BUT THE MOST POWERFUL OF ALL WAS THE DRAGON!!
THE DRAGON WITH EIGHT HEADS!!

KRSSSH
IT IS OVER ....
WUM
HIS POWER IS FAR TOO TERRIBLE TO SURVIVE ...

A HUMAN CANNOT TAME THE SUN...
RECCA DOES NOT HAVE THE STRENGTH TO MASTER IT....

WHAM
FORGET HER! SAVE YOUR-SELF!
WHAT ABOUT THE GIRL!?
RUN! IT'S COLLAPSING !!
AAAAH !!
KRASH
...
...
AAAAH AAAAH
UMF ....
DARN THESE ...
HEH ... HEH .....
YOU WILL BURN TO DEATH!!
ROOAAARR
YOUR SKILLS MEAN NOTHING NOW! YOU'LL BE BUFFETED, THEN CONSUMED BY THAT FLAME!!
HA HA HA HA! YOU PATHETIC FOOL!

REC ...
RECCA ...
PRINCESS ...
GRAAAR
WHOOSH
!!

STOP! YOU IDIOT!!

STOP OR I'LL KILL YOU!!

Part Thirty-Six: The Big Exit

Part Thirty-Six:
The Big Exit

THE DRAGON ...
SPOKE!

!!

I COMMANDED YOU! GOT A PROBLEM WITH THAT!!
IF YOU SINGE ONE HAIR ON PRINCESS'S HEAD, I'LL WRING YOUR NECK!!

HOW CAN HE BE SO FEARLESS?
IS HE TOO STUPID TO COMPREHEND THE DANGER?

WE ARE FREE FROM YOUR TEKKŌ!
YET YOU DARE TO GIVE US, THE EIGHT-HEADED DRAGON, COMMANDS?

ROOO
YOU GOT IT!
YOU GUYS WERE INSIDE OF ME, RIGHT! THAT MAKES ME YOUR LANDLORD!

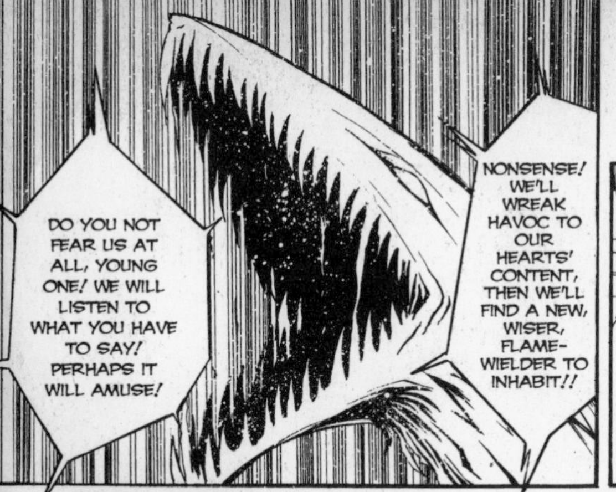
NONSENSE! WE'LL WREAK HAVOC TO OUR HEARTS' CONTENT, THEN WE'LL FIND A NEW, WISER, FLAME-WIELDER TO INHABIT!!
DO YOU NOT FEAR US AT ALL, YOUNG ONE! WE WILL LISTEN TO WHAT YOU HAVE TO SAY! PERHAPS IT WILL AMUSE!

HA HA HA
HO HO HO

THEN, WE WILL DO WITH YOU AS WE PLEASE.

RESHIN!
COME, LET ME HAVE MY FUN!

IF I AM PLEASED WITH YOUR OFFERING, I SHALL LEND YOU A HAND JUST ONCE.
NOW TELL ME! WHAT DO YOU OFFER?

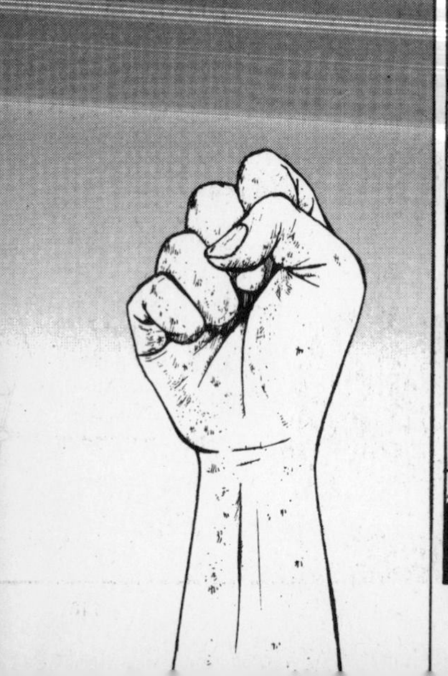

ONE ARM!

THERE'S A BAD GUY I NEED TO BEAT.
...

HE KILLS PEOPLE JUST TO HAVE HIS WAY.
HE MURDERS WOMEN AND CHILDREN WITH A SMILE ON HIS FACE.

WHAT A COOL OLD HOUSE!!

THIS IS KAGEHOSHI'S HOUSE? WOW!!
BLAB
IT'S THREE TIMES THE SIZE OF MY PLACE.
SO FAR FROM CIVILIZATION... CREEPY.
LOOK, THERE ARE KOI IN THE POND! ♡
BLAB
LOOK, THERE ARE KOI IN THE POND!

THIS WAS USED AS A HIDING GROUND FOR THE HOKAGE IN THE PAST. A FORCE-FIELD SURROUNDS IT.
NORMALLY YOU WOULD NOT BE ABLE TO ENTER. IT SHOULDN'T BE DETECTED BY KUREI'S PEOPLE TOO EASILY.

THE HOKAGE REALLY EXISTED!!
MS. KAGE-HOSHI, THIS IS AMAZING!!!

RECCA'S TEACHER, MR. TATE-SAKO.
LIKE RECCA, A NINJA FANATIC, WITH A PARTICULAR INTEREST IN THE HOKAGE CLAN.

HEY!
THWAK
BUMP BUMP BUMP BUMP
WHAT ARE YOU DOING HERE!?
C'MON, RECCA!
I GOTTA HEAR THE SECRETS OF THE HOKAGE, TOO! ♡

YOU GUYS TOO!!
IT SOUNDED LIKE FUN. GOT A PROBLEM WITH THAT?
I CAME 'CAUSE FUKO CAME!! GOT A PROBLEM WITH THAT?
I DON'T KNOW WHY I'M HERE.
GRRR
I'LL LEAVE IF YOU WANT.
DON'T BOTHER TO LOOK FOR ME IF I GET LOST.
AAAH! NOT YOU PRINCESS! ♡
IT'S ALL RIGHT. ALL OF YOU SHOULD HEAR WHAT I HAVE TO SAY.
PLEASE COME INSIDE ....

HEY, RECCA! ARE YOU SURE WE CAN TRUST HER!?
SHE'S KINDA WEIRD.
MRF?
PLUM TEA...
KRUNCH KRUNCH
TEA COOKIE
WEIRD, YEAH, BUT THERE'S *SOME-THING* ABOUT HER.
I'M GONNA HEAR HER OUT!
EXCUSE ME.
HSSSK...
WELCOME ...
I AM KAGEHOSHI, LADY OF THIS MANOR.

MY NAME IS NOT KAGEHOSHI ...

IT IS KAGERŌ!

M-ME AND KUREI ....
BROTHERS !?

THAT KUREI!? THE EVIL GUY!?
SO IF HE'S FOUR YEARS OLDER AND WE'RE SIXTEEN...
WHOA! HE'S TWENTY NOW!
HMMM
SO, THE CLAN WASN'T ENTIRELY DEPENDENT ON THEIR TALISMANS! THEY HAD A FLAME-WIELDER LEADING THEM!
PLEASE CONTINUE, KAGEHO- I MEAN, KAGERŌ!

REINA ARGUED THAT KUREI WAS THE RIGHTFUL HEIR.

THOUGH HE IS THE SECOND HEIR, KUREI WHO WAS OKA'S FIRST BORN!

THE NEXT HEAD OF HOKAGE SHALL BE KUREI!!

REINA ...

KUREI IS THE HEIR! RECCA IS ACCURSED! HE SHOULD BE KILLED!!

STOP !!

THE REAL CURSED IS ON...

KUREI!!

WHAT !?
HOW CAN YOU SAY THAT, LORD OOJIJI!! HOW DARE YOU DEFAME KUREI, THE TRUE HEIR!!
DO YOU KNOW WHY I ALLOWED ANOTHER HEIR EVEN AFTER KUREI'S BIRTH?
I SENSED SOMETHING IN THAT CHILD.

AN EVIL SOUL!
A CURSED FLAME!!

WE DO NOT NEED TWO CHILDREN OF THE FLAME...
SRIK---
KUREI MUST DIE!
NO ...
HOW CAN YOU...
WHAT HAS KUREI DONE?
NOOOOO!!
WAIT!

LORD OOJIJI...
IT IS INAPPROPRIATE FOR A SHINOBI TO MURDER A CHILD.
I BEG YOU... SPARE KUREI.
SOON...
A YEAR HAD PASSED...
YOU ARE CURSED, KUREI!!
LEAVE THIS VILLAGE!
DIE!!
WUP
KOFF KOFF
POOR KUREI... YOU SHOULD HAVE BEEN THE ONE TO BECOME OUR LEADER...
IF ONLY RECCA WASN'T HERE... IF ONLY!
MOTHER, IF RECCA WERE TO DIE...
WOULD THAT END OUR SUFFERING?

GOO GOO
GA GA

IF HE DIES...

WAAAAH

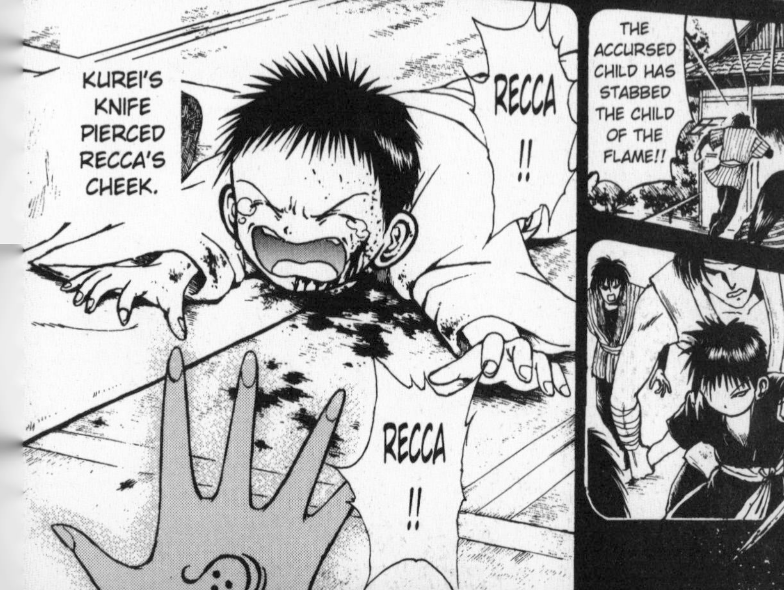
THE ACCURSED CHILD!!
THE ACCURSED CHILD HAS STABBED THE CHILD OF THE FLAME!!
RECCA!!
RECCA!!
KUREI'S KNIFE PIERCED RECCA'S CHEEK.

HA HA HA! CRY! SUFFER!! DIE!!
BECAUSE OF YOU, MOTHER AND I ARE OUTCASTS! YOU ARE THE CAUSE OF ALL OUR MISERY!!
DON'T YOU REMEMBER? I GAVE YOU THAT!
...
TINGLE...
KUREI WAS ONLY FIVE AT THE TIME?
WHAT A PSYCHO ...
LUCKY IT WAS THE CHEEK.
HE COULD'VE BEEN KILLED.
CHOMP CHOMP
KRUNCH
HYA HA HA HA HA HA HA!!
I'M GOING TO MEET SOMEONE I NEVER EXPECTED TO SEE AGAIN !!!

COME ON!! DO YOU GUYS REALLY BELIEVE THIS!?

400 YEARS AGO? THEN HOW DID I GET HERE, NOW!!!

YOU DRIFTED THROUGH TIME...

LET ME EXPLAIN.

HEH... I KNEW THERE WAS SOMETHING INTERESTING BEHIND THAT FORCE-FIELD.

IT'S A HIDE OUT!!

WE SANBAGARASU WILL TAKE POSSESSION OF IT!

IT'LL MAKE FOR A GREAT GIFT TO KUREI!

RESHIN!

IT'S DIRTY AND SLIGHTLY USED, BUT IT'S ALL YOURS!

JUST FOR ME?

WUMP...

EVERYBODY WAS HURT... JUST TO SAVE ME.

I WANT TO DO MY PART.

MR. RESHIN, PLEASE, HELP RECCA.

PRINCESS!

YOU CAN HAVE *MY* ARM INSTEAD!

THEN TAKE MISS FUKO'S LEG, TOO!
HOLD ON THERE!

CONSIDERING HACKING THE DRAGON INTO SASHIMI AT THE FIRST OPPORTUNITY.
...

SHUT UP, YOU MORONS!! THIS HAS NOTHING TO DO WITH YOU GUYS!
RECCA'S RIGHT ...

!
OUR DEAL WAS FOR ONE ARM.
HOWEVER, I'LL FORGIVE YOUR DEBT, JUST THIS ONCE.

YOU'RE AN ENTERTAINING LITTLE FELLOW... I WISH TO SEE MORE OF YOUR BATTLES.

WE WISH TO HAVE YOU AS OUR RESTING PLACE ONCE MORE.

BUT WHEN THE DAY COMES THAT YOU LOSE...
WOOSH
AND IT WON'T JUST BE YOUR ARM. I SHALL TAKE YOUR ENTIRE BODY!
FWASH
FWASH
UNTIL THEN, POLISH THAT ARM OF YOURS.
KHWRRR
IMPRES-SIVE...
KRAAK
WHOA!!
YOU COMMANDED THE FLAME DRAGON!
YOU DEFEATED KUREI!!
HOLD ON...
IT WASN'T JUST ME!

I HAD THESE GUYS.
GET IT OFF OF ME!!
WHY DIDN'T YOU ESCAPE !?
FUKO!
IT'S MR. TATESAKO !!
HEY, MR. TATE-SAKO!!
YEEEK
GANKO !?
ZZZZ
THANK GOD...
HE'S ALIVE !!

GOOD JOB, GANKO! DID YOU RESCUE HIM!?
GEEZ, JUST LOOK AT THIS MESS!
SKRUFF
SKRUFF
NO.
KAORU SAVED US.
THAT TOUGH LITTLE ...
KID !?
KAORU ...
I KNEW HE WAS A NICE PERSON!
WHOA !!?

KRAK
UH-OH, THIS PLACE IS COLLAPSING!
BECAUSE OF THE DAMAGE *YOU* CAUSE!
RM
MB
LET'S GET THE HECK OUTTA HERE!!
WUP
STOP
STAY, DOMON. YOU COULD SWEAT OFF A FEW TONS.

RM
MB

LOOK AT IT BURN ...
I WONDER IF YANAGI'S ALL RIGHT ...
TMP...
!
KAORU... IS THAT YOU?

WHAT ARE YOU DOING HERE?

RAIHA!
NEON !
JISHO!
AND EVEN GENJURO!

AND ...
KUREI !

ALL FOUR MEMBERS OF KUREI'S ASSASSIN GROUP URUHA!
FWAP
PLANNING TO INVADE AMERICA OR SOMETHING?

I NEED TO TALK TO YOU GUYS ANYWAYS.
KRK...
I THOUGHT I MIGHT FIND YOU HERE.

I CAN'T WORK FOR YOU ANYMORE!
CONSIDER THIS MY RESIGNATION!!

I...
BELIEVED IN YOU.
...
YOU'RE A MERE CHILD, AFTER ALL...

MY, MY, KAORU.♪ WHAT A NAUGHTY BOY YOU ARE.♡
YOU DESERVE A SOUND THRASHING. ♡
NO, NEON! HE'S JUST A KID!!
THINK IT OVER, KAORU!! I DON'T WANT YOU TO DIE!!
HO HO
THE YOUNGER YOU ARE, THE MORE CROSS-ROADS YOU MUST FACE...
HO HO
SUCH IS LIFE.
NO.
LEAVE HIM BE!
I HAD GREAT PLANS FOR YOU, KAORU...
BUT SOME FRUIT ROTS ON THE VINE.

I'M HUNGRY.
THAT'S FOR SURE.
...
SOME-BODY ...
HA
SHE'S SOMETHING ELSE!!
BWAHAHAHA
HUH ?
THEY THINK IT IS OVER..
BUT ...
THIS WAS MERELY THE BEGINNING.

RECCA AND THE OTHERS INFILTRATED KUREI'S MANSION TO RESCUE YANAGI AND MR. TATESAKO.
AFTER SEVERAL FIERCE BATTLES, THEY NARROWLY DEFEATED KUREI AND SAVED THE HOSTAGES.

NOW ...
RECCA, AS I SAID BEFORE, I HAVE SOMETHING TO TELL YOU.
WILL YOU LISTEN?
THE TIME HAS COME FOR ALL THE MYSTERIES TO BE REVEALED ...

AFTER YANAGI USES HER POWERS TO HEAL TATESAKO'S WIFE...
THEY TRAVEL TO A REMOTE MOUNTAIN.

Part Thirty-Eight:

The Secret History 1

WHAT A COOL OLD HOUSE!!

THIS IS KAGEHOSHI'S HOUSE? WOW!!
IT'S THREE TIMES THE SIZE OF MY PLACE.
BLAB
SO FAR FROM CIVILIZATION... CREEPY.
LOOK, THERE ARE KOI IN THE POND! ♡
BLAB
LOOK, THERE ARE KOI IN THE POND!

THIS WAS USED AS A HIDING GROUND FOR THE HOKAGE IN THE PAST. A FORCE-FIELD SURROUNDS IT.
NORMALLY YOU WOULD NOT BE ABLE TO ENTER. IT SHOULDN'T BE DETECTED BY KUREI'S PEOPLE TOO EASILY.

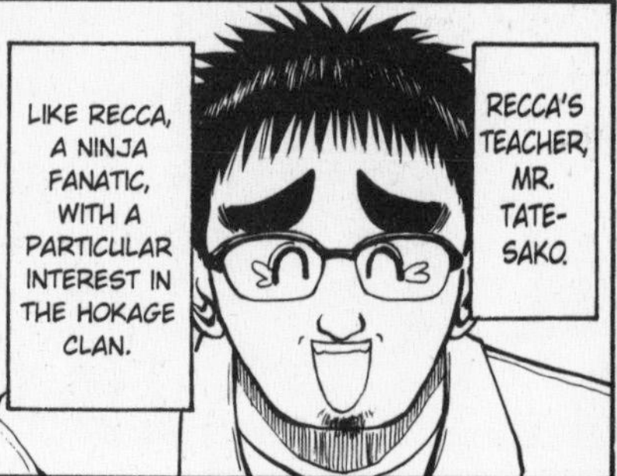
RECCA'S TEACHER, MR. TATE-SAKO.
LIKE RECCA, A NINJA FANATIC, WITH A PARTICULAR INTEREST IN THE HOKAGE CLAN.

MS. KAGE-HOSHI, THIS IS AMAZING!!!
THE HOKAGE REALLY EXISTED!!

C'MON, RECCA!
I GOTTA HEAR THE SECRETS OF THE HOKAGE, TOO! ♡
WHAT ARE YOU DOING HERE!?
THWAK
BUMP BUMP BUMP
HEY!

IT'S ALL RIGHT. ALL OF YOU SHOULD HEAR WHAT I HAVE TO SAY.

PLEASE COME INSIDE....

YOU GUYS TOO!!

IT SOUNDED LIKE FUN. GOT A PROBLEM WITH THAT?

I CAME 'CAUSE FUKO CAME!! GOT A PROBLEM WITH THAT?

I DON'T KNOW WHY I'M HERE.

GRRR

AAAH! NOT YOU PRINCESS! ♡

I'LL LEAVE IF YOU WANT.

DON'T BOTHER TO LOOK FOR ME IF I GET LOST.

HEY, RECCA! ARE YOU SURE WE CAN TRUST HER!?
SHE'S KINDA WEIRD.
MRF?
TEA COOKIE
KRUNCH KRUNCH
PLUM TEA...
WEIRD, YEAH, BUT THERE'S SOMETHING ABOUT HER.
I'M GONNA HEAR HER OUT!
EXCUSE ME.
HSSSK...
WELCOME...
I AM KAGEHOSHI, LADY OF THIS MANOR.

MY NAME IS NOT KAGEHOSHI ...

IT IS KAGERŌ!

I AM YOUR MOTHER.

IN THE SENGOKU PERIOD, THE SHINOBI CLANS FLOURISHED IN A TIME OF CEASELESS CIVIL WAR.

THE IGA CLAN

THE KOGA CLAN

THE HYUMA CLAN

AND THE HOKAGE CLAN!

THOSE WHO WERE TO BECOME THE LEADERS OF THE HOKAGE POSSESSED A UNIQUE GIFT.
THE POWER OF FLAME!

ITS ORIGIN IS UNKNOWN... BUT THE GIFT WAS PASSED FROM ONE GENERATION TO THE NEXT.

THE SIXTH HEAD OF THE HOKAGE
OKA, THE FLAME-WIELDER

IS IT HERE YET!? THE BABY!?
OW !!
OOF
OUR CHILD IS BORN!?
KAGERŌ !?

YES, LORD OKA...

A STRONG BOY.

OKA WAS THE FATHER...

KAGERŌ THE MOTHER...

ONLY ONE CHILD OF THE FLAMES SHOULD APPEAR IN EACH GENERATION TO BECOME OUR LEADER!
BUT NOW THERE ARE TWO!!

KAGERŌ'S CHILD, THE FIRST HEIR BORN YESTERDAY, RECCA!!

REINA'S CHILD, THE SECOND HEIR, KUREI!!

THE BIRTH OF A CHILD OF THE FLAME WAS A MUCH HOPED FOR EVENT...
FLAME-WIELDERS OFTEN TOOK TWO OR THREE WIVES.

KUREI WAS RECCA'S HALF-BROTHER.
HE WAS FOUR YEARS OLD WHEN RECCA WAS BORN.

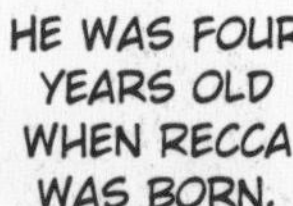

M-ME AND KUREI ....
BROTHERS !?

THAT KUREI!? THE EVIL GUY!?
SO IF HE'S FOUR YEARS OLDER AND WE'RE SIXTEEN...
WHOA! HE'S TWENTY NOW!
HMMM

SO, THE CLAN WASN'T ENTIRELY DEPENDENT ON THEIR TALISMANS! THEY HAD A FLAME-WIELDER LEADING THEM!
PLEASE CONTINUE, KAGEHO- I MEAN, KAGERŌ!

REINA ARGUED THAT KUREI WAS THE RIGHTFUL HEIR.

THOUGH HE IS THE SECOND HEIR, KUREI WHO WAS OKA'S FIRST BORN!

THE NEXT HEAD OF HOKAGE SHALL BE KUREI!!

KUREI IS THE HEIR! RECCA IS ACCURSED! HE SHOULD BE KILLED!!

REINA ...

STOP !!

THE REAL CURSED IS ON...

KUREI!!

WHAT !?
HOW CAN YOU SAY THAT, LORD OOJIJI!! HOW DARE YOU DEFAME KUREI, THE TRUE HEIR!!
DO YOU KNOW WHY I ALLOWED ANOTHER HEIR EVEN AFTER KUREI'S BIRTH?
I SENSED SOMETHING IN THAT CHILD.

AN EV
SOUL
A CURSED FLAME!!

SRIK...
WE DO NOT NEED TWO CHILDREN OF THE FLAME...
KUREI MUST DIE!
NO...
HOW CAN YOU...
WHAT HAS KUREI DONE?
NOOOOO!!
WAIT!

LORD OOJIJI ...
IT IS INAPPROPRIATE FOR A SHINOBI TO MURDER A CHILD.
I BEG YOU... SPARE KUREI.
SOON...
A YEAR HAD PASSED...
YOU ARE CURSED, KUREI!!
LEAVE THIS VILLAGE!
DIE!!
WUP
KOFF KOFF
POOR KUREI... YOU SHOULD HAVE BEEN THE ONE TO BECOME OUR LEADER...
IF ONLY RECCA WASN'T HERE... IF ONLY!
MOTHER, IF RECCA WERE TO DIE...
WOULD THAT END OUR SUFFERING?

GOO GOO
GA GA
IF HE DIES...
WAAAAH
THE ACCURSED CHILD!!
THE ACCURSED CHILD HAS STABBED THE CHILD OF THE FLAME!!
RECCA !!
RECCA !!
KUREI'S KNIFE PIERCED RECCA'S CHEEK.

HA HA HA! CRY! SUFFER!! DIE!!
BECAUSE OF YOU, MOTHER AND I ARE OUTCASTS! YOU ARE THE CAUSE OF ALL OUR MISERY!!
...
DON'T YOU REMEMBER? I GAVE YOU THAT!
TINGLE...
KUREI WAS ONLY FIVE AT THE TIME?
WHAT A PSYCHO ...
LUCKY IT WAS THE CHEEK.
HE COULD'VE BEEN KILLED.
KRUNCH
CHOMP CHOMP
DELAY
REACTI
HYA HA HA HA HA HA HA!!
I'M GOING TO MEET SOMEONE I NEVER EXPECTED TO SEE AGAIN!!!

400 YEARS AGO? THEN HOW DID I GET HERE, NOW!!!

COME ON!! DO YOU GUYS REALLY BELIEVE THIS!?

LET ME EXPLAIN.

YOU DRIFTED THROUGH TIME...

HEH... I KNEW THERE WAS SOMETHING INTERESTING BEHIND THAT FORCE-FIELD.

IT'S A HIDE OUT!!

WE SANBAGARASU WILL TAKE POSSESSION OF IT!

IT'LL MAKE FOR A GREAT GIFT TO KUREI!

THIRD YEAR OF THE TENSHŌ ERA
AFTER KUREI'S ATTEMPTED ASSASSINATION OF RECCA---
HE WAS CONFINED TO A CELL.
KLUNK
IT'S FOOD.
EAT IT...
DON'T WANT IT?
UNGRATEFUL WHELP.
WELL, I GUESS I'D BE ANGRY TOO.
MY MOTHER?
YOUR MOTHER WAS FREED OF RESPONSIBILITY IN THE MATTER.
BUT YOU WILL NEVER LEAVE THIS CELL ALIVE, I'M AFRAID.

NOBUNAGA ODA OF OWARI...
IS SENDING HIS ARMIES AGAINST US!!

TEN THOUSAND SOLDIERS ARE HEADED THIS WAY ...
THE INTEL-LIGENCE IS RELIABLE, I GOT IT FROM THE LIPS OF OUR SPY!
THE FOOL FROM OWARI! HE WANTS OUR TALISMANS!
THEY WILL ASSURE HIS CONQUEST OF THE ENTIRE REALM!
PLACE THE TALISMANS IN HERE!!
TUMP....
HERE, TAKE THE KOGONANKI!
WE'LL SHOW THAT FOOL!
STOP !!
WE WON'T BE USING ANY TALISMANS!!
OKA-- THE SIXTH LEADER OF THE HOKAGE

LORD OKA !!
WE ARE OUT NUMBERED! WE NEED THE TALISMANS!!
THEY ARE TEN THOUSAND! EVEN IF WE DRIVE THEM OFF, THEY ARE ALMOST CERTAIN TO CAPTURE SOME OF OUR TALISMANS, AND NOBUNAGA WILL USE THEM AGAINST US!!
WE COULD NOT DEFEAT HIS ARMIES AND OUR OWN TALISMANS. AND THE WHOLE WORLD WILL FALL TO CHAOS!
LISTEN! THIS IS NOT JUST A HOKAGE BATTLE!
GRUMBLE
GRUMBLE
IT IS A BATTLE TO SAVE THE REALM!!!
OKA...
I WON'T LET HIM HAVE EVEN ONE TALISMAN !!
AND BY KILLING ME, NOBUNAGA WILL FRUSTRATE HIS OWN DESIGN!

HEH
HA HA HA ....
A HOLY MISSION TO PROTECT THE REALM! SPLENDID!!
HAH! WE NEED NO MAGIC CHARMS TO DEFEAT THOSE SWINE!
HMM HMM
ALL RIGHT! HIDE THE TALISMANS !!!

THE HOKAGE MADOGU... ITS POWER ATTRACTED THE DEVIL HIMSELF.
MAYBE IT SHOULD HAVE NEVER EXISTED...
...

MY PEOPLE ...
YOU HAVE MY GRATITUDE!

THEY'RE HERE!
IT'S ODA!
PUOO AAAP

I'M SORRY... KAGERŌ ...
I WAS A BAD HUSBAND.

I FAILED AT EVERY-THING ...
FOR RECCA TOO...

GOODBYE.

NO. AS A SHINOBI, AS OUR LEADER, YOU WERE GREAT.
I AM PROUD TO BE YOUR WIFE.

I LOVE YOU ...

I AM ENJUTSUSHI OKA, LEADER OF THE HOKAGE CLAN!!
WOOSH
THOSE WHO ARE READY TO DEPART THIS WORLD, STEP FORWARD!!!

THIS HAND OF FLAME ...
BEARS THE BLOOD OF COUNTLESS BATTLES...
RECCA ...
KUREI ...
I WAS FORTUNATE TO HAVE HELD YOU BOTH WITH THIS HAND.
I WAS FORTUNATE ...
OKA, KILLED IN BATTLE, AGE 32.

THEN ...

DON'T BE AFRAID, RECCA...

I'LL GET YOU TO A SAFE PLACE...

KAGERŌ, THERE IS A SECRET POWER A HOKAGE MUST NEVER USE...
THE POWER TO CROSS TIME!!
NO ONE MAY VIOLATE THE LAWS OF TIME! YOU WOULD BECOME BOUND IN TIME IF YOU DID.
BOUND IN TIME ?
IMMORTAL. YOU COULD NEVER DIE !!

YOU MUST CONTINUE TO LIVE AND WATCH THE BIRTH AND DEATH OF THOSE YOU LOVE...
IT IS TORMENT TO BE UNABLE TO PASS FROM THIS VALE OF TEARS...
BE WARNED!

IF YOU LIVE ...
WE'LL MEET AGAIN ...

RIN
HEI
ZAI
TOU
SHA
KAI
JIN
ZEN
RETSU

FWASH
SPACE-TIME DRIFT!!!
I WILL NOT LET THIS CHILD DIE!!

TAKE GOOD CARE OF THIS TEKKŌ I MADE...
IT WILL PROTECT YOU...
GOODBYE ...
RECCA ...
IT'S EXACTLY LIKE...
THE DREAM I HAD AT KUREI'S MANSION!!
SHW
RRR
KUREI !!?
WAAAAAA !?
!!?
WHAT ARE YOU DOING HERE!?
HIS PRISON WAS OPENED IN THE BATTLE ...
KUREI WILL DRIFT ACROSS TIME AS WELL!
RECCA.
KUREI !!
SWUP

CHUNK

THE BATTLE LASTED ONE NIGHT...

ONE ROSE TO ITS FEET.
AMID THE HUN-DREDS OF CORPSES...

OOOOO
ITS HEART HAD BEEN PIERCED...
BUT NO TRACE OF THE WOUND REMAINED.

A MOTHER HAD BROKEN THE LAWS OF TIME AND DOOMED HERSELF TO ETERNAL LIFE.
HER NAME WAS KAGERŌ.

THAT NIGHT I ABANDONED THE NAME "KAGERO," AND CALLED MYSELF "KAGE-HOSHI."

THEN I DRIFTED, TO EDO, MEIJI, TAISHO LOOKING FOR THE CHILD I HAD CAST UPON THE WATERS OF TIME. FOR FOUR HUNDRED YEARS I SEARCHED.

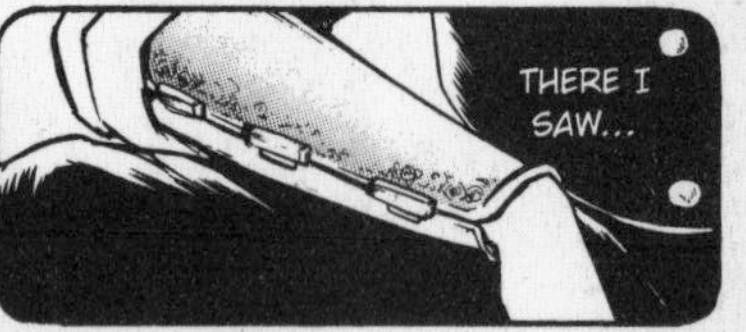

KUREI MUST HAVE DRIFTED TO THE SAME ERA... THOUGH THE TWO HAD NOT SEEMED TO HAVE MET YET...

HEY, OLD LADY...

WHO ARE YOU?

IT WAS DANGEROUS... KUREI MIGHT HAVE DISCOVERED RECCA'S PRESCENCE IF I GOT TOO NEAR TO HIM...

MR. HANABISHI, SHE'S NOT OLD!!

AND I KNEW HE WOULD NOT YET BELIEVE MY STORY...

FINE. I'LL PLAY YOUR GAME

TAA!

WUNK

SO I MOLDED EVENTS AROUND YOU.

SW

AP

TOO LATE!!

THE WOUNDS MAY BE SHALLOW, BUT YOU'RE LOSING BLOOD!! YOU COULD DIE.

THAT IS WHY I FIRST APPROACHED YOU WEARING A MASK OF EVIL!

I GAVE FUJIN TO MISS KIRISAWA, AND SENT MIKAGAMI TO FIGHT YOU!

BELIEVING YOU WOULDN'T LOSE,

BELIEVING THEY WOULD JOIN YOU IN YOUR FIGHT AGAINST KUREI!!

...
REALLY ?
WHAT'S UP, TOKIYA?
CAN'T YOU FEEL THEIR PRESENCE?
WUP
THREE OF THEM.
KRASH
TO BE CONTINUED!!

My Picture Diary: Zero Tsu (expert)

I DON'T USUALLY WATCH TV DURING WORK. I NEVER REALLY ENJOYED IT, SO IT'S FINE

DURING WORK I PLAY MUSIC. 99% OF IT FROM THE RADIO.

THESE ARE SOME OF THE SONGS I'VE BEEN LISTENING TO: TETSUDOU SHONEN NO IKOI

TETSUDOU SHONEN NO IKOI
KOINU NI SHITEAGERU > KINNIKU SHOJO TAI
SKATEBOYS / BRAND NEW MONKEYS
STAFOLOS NO TATAKAI /GUIN SAGA HENKYŌ HEN
RESET
BURA BURA > SUGIMOTO KYŌICHI
WARUKUNAI YOKUNAI / TOMOVSKY
4 PLUGS (ALBUM) /THE MAD CAPSULE MARKETS

INOUE SHOKO (HOTTIE)
ALSO INOUE SHOKO'S "JUNSHIN." I USUALLY HATE LOVE SONGS AND BALLADS BUT I REALLY LIKE THIS ONE.

BUT IT SEEMS LIKE MY EX-ASSISTANT PIKEEN SHIMIZU IS INTO IT WAY MORE THAN I AM.
PLAY "JUNSHIN," MAN, "JUNSHIN"!!
IT RULES!
PUT IT ON REPEAT, REPEAT GYAHAHA HA!!
SHUT UP.
LIKES TO SING ALONG. WHAT A CREEP.

TBS IS THE STATION I LISTEN TO MOST.

IJUUIN HIKARU NO UPS

MIYAKAWA MASARU NO DARE NANDA OMAE WA

AND OTHERS.

NO GRAFFITI
BY THE WAY ...

THE RADIO SHOW I LOVED MOST WAS ...
"TUNNELS NO ALL NIGHT NIPPON" !!
DON'T ASK WHY...

STUDENTS THESE DAYS MAY NOT KNOW IT, BUT I USED TO LISTEN TO THE SHOW WHILE STRUGGLING TO STAY AWAKE.
SHAVED HEAD FOR KENDO CLUB

I'D LOVE TO HEAR IT AGAIN!
JUST AS I WAS THINKING THAT...

HAYASHI, WHO HELPED ME OUT ONCE...
I'VE GOT SOME "TUNNELS" ON TAPE!
LENT ME ABOUT 10 TAPES OF IT!
WOW!

I LISTENED TO IT EVERY DAY!
BUT HUMANS ARE INSATIABLE CREATURES

I'M BORED!
I WANT NEW ONES!

SO HERE'S MY REQUEST !!

PLEASE RESPOND BY LETTER.

ANY OF YOU OUT THERE WHO HAVE ANY "TUNNELS" TAPES TO GIVE! (DENKI GROOVE WILL DO, TOO.)
ANY OUT THERE? I'LL COMPENS-ATE YOU FOR THEM!!!

(THE FOLLOWING IS RUN-CHAN'S 3RD EPISODE)
THANKS TO THE PEOPLE WHO'VE SENT STUFF IN. BUT IT MAY END REAL SOON (I'M GETTING BORED OF IT).
NEXT ISSUE, THE FINAL EPISODE!?

ANYBODY WITH "TUNNELS," THE NOW NEARLY EXTINCT COMEDY SKETCH TAPE "MASHIO"?

Magical Girl Run-chan

► EPISODE 3 ◄

THE SILK HAT LEFT BEHIND

WHAT WILL RUN-CHAN DO!

CONSIDERING HER OPTIONS

① WEAR IT

② THROW IT AWAY

③ OTHER

烈火の炎
~FLAME OF RECCA~

Team Hokage Recommendations

If you like Flame of Recca, here are three more books worth checking out:

Vagabond: The continuing saga of a young samurai on his quest to become the best swordsman in Japan. Unarguably, one of the most beautifully illustrated comics in the world.

InuYasha: Myths and legends come alive when a teenage girl finds herself trapped in an ancient Japanese fairy tale.

Revolutionary Girl Utena: Armed with the Sword of Dios and the passion of her convictions, Utena Tenjou revolutionizes the world. Adolescence was never so iconic.

BEAUTY AND THE BEAK?

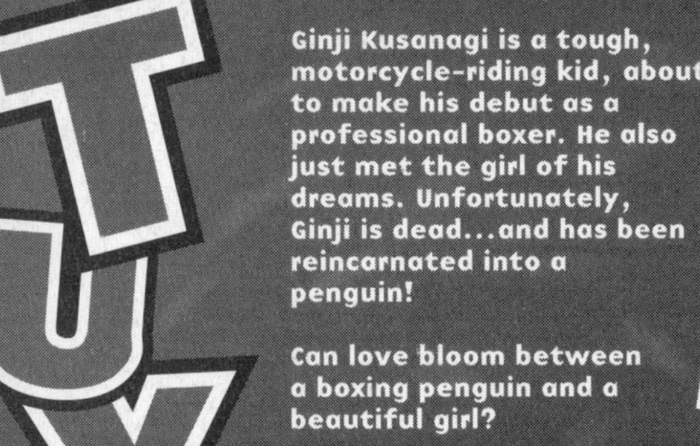

Ginji Kusanagi is a tough, motorcycle-riding kid, about to make his debut as a professional boxer. He also just met the girl of his dreams. Unfortunately, Ginji is dead...and has been reincarnated into a penguin!

Can love bloom between a boxing penguin and a beautiful girl?

COLLECT THE GRAPHIC NOVELS TODAY!

www.viz.com